KID'S ROCK Drum Method
by Dawn Richardson

Online Audio www.melbay.com/22022BCDEB

Audio contents

1	Page 11; Ex. 1	21	Page 20; Ex. 6	41	Page 29; Ex. 2	61	Page 40; Ex. 4	81	Page 48; Ex. 3
2	Page 12; Ex. 1	22	Page 21; Ex. 2	42	Page 29; Ex. 3	62	Page 40; Ex. 5	82	Page 48; Ex. 4
3	Page 12; Ex. 3	23	Page 21; Ex. 4	43	Page 31; Ex. 1	63	Page 40; Ex. 6	83	Page 49; Ex. 1
4	Page 12; Ex. 5	24	Page 21; Ex. 5	44	Page 32; Ex. 1	64	Page 41; Ex. 1	84	Page 49; Ex. 4
5	Page 13; Ex. 1	25	Page 23; Ex. 1	45	Page 32; Ex. 2	65	Page 41; Ex. 3	85	Page 49; Ex. 5
6	Page 13; Ex. 2	26	Page 23; Ex. 3	46	Page 32; Ex. 3	66	Page 41; Ex. 4	86	Page 51; Ex. 1
7	Page 13; Ex. 3	27	Page 23; Ex. 5	47	Page 32; Ex. 4	67	Page 41; Ex. 6	87	Page 51; Ex. 3
8	Page 15; Ex. 1	28	Page 24; Ex. 1	48	Page 32; Ex. 5	68	Page 43; Ex. 1	88	Page 51; Ex. 5
9	Page 15; Ex. 2	29	Page 24; Ex. 3	49	Page 32; Ex. 6	69	Page 43; Ex. 3	89	Page 51; Ex. 6
10	Page 15; Ex. 3	30	Page 24; Ex. 5	50	Page 33; Ex. 1	70	Page 44; Ex. 1	90	Page 52; Ex. 1
11	Page 16; Ex. 1	31	Page 24; Ex. 6	51	Page 33; Ex. 2	71	Page 44; Ex. 3	91	Page 52; Ex. 3
12	Page 16; Ex. 2	32	Page 25; Ex. 2	52	Page 33; Ex. 3	72	Page 44; Ex. 5	92	Page 53; Ex. 1
13	Page 16; Ex. 3	33	Page 25; Ex. 4	53	Page 35; Ex. 1	73	Page 45; Ex. 1	93	Page 53; Ex. 3
14	Page 17; Solo	34	Page 25; Ex. 5	54	Page 35; Ex. 4	74	Page 45; Ex. 3	94	Page 54; Ex. 1
15	Page 19; Ex. 1	35	Page 27; Ex. 1	55	Page 36; Ex. 1	75	Page 45; Ex. 4	95	Page 54; Ex. 3
16	Page 19; Ex. 3	36	Page 28; Ex. 1	56	Page 36; Ex. 2	76	Page 47; Ex. 2	96	Page 54; Ex. 5
17	Page 19; Ex. 5	37	Page 28; Ex. 2	57	Page 37; Solo	77	Page 47; Ex. 3	97	Page 55; Ex. 1
18	Page 20; Ex. 1	38	Page 28; Ex. 3	58	Page 39; Ex. 1	78	Page 47; Ex. 4	98	Page 56; Ex. 1
19	Page 20; Ex. 3	39	Page 28; Ex. 5	59	Page 40; Ex. 2	79	Page 48; Ex. 1		
20	Page 20; Ex. 4	40	Page 29; Ex. 1	60	Page 40; Ex. 3	80	Page 48; Ex. 2		

1 2 3 4 5 6 7 8 9 0

Visit us on the Web at www.melbay.com — E-mail us at email@melbay.com

Foreword

After teaching private drum lessons for many years to students of all ages, I began to take note of concepts and methods that seemed to work better for my younger students and eventually compiled them into this text. This book is directed toward the very young learner, approximately 4 – 8 years old. I found the larger text and larger staff size helpful and that less information on each page also seemed to make learning easier for my young students. Amazingly, I experienced kids that were not yet able to even read words could learn to read and count quarter notes and many more note values. They could learn not only to count, but also to do basic patterns on the drum kit at a very young age. I found it helpful to balance hands-only work with the drum kit and did my best to include practice and exercises for both in almost every chapter of this text to keep it interesting and exciting for the student. It's been a great journey and I thank all of my students for helping me learn so much more about drumming and teaching me how to continue to help others learn. Drums are a fun instrument and learning notation and counting gives all of my young students a well-deserved sense of accomplishment and the tools to practice at home. I hope this text can serve to introduce more young students to drumming and help instructors looking for the tools to teach this particular age group.

About the Author

Dawn holds her Bachelor of Arts Degree in Percussion from Cal State Los Angeles and has studied with the principal percussionist of the Los Angeles Philharmonic, *Raynor Carroll* and with studio greats *Steve Houghton* and *Greg Goodall*. She has played drums and percussion in all sorts of groups including rock bands, marching band, concert band, orchestra and percussion ensembles. Dawn currently lives in San Francisco where she continues to teach, write, perform and record with various musical projects.

Dawn has toured and/or recorded with *Tracy Chapman; 4 Non Blondes; Shana Morrison; Joe Gore; Penelope Houston; Angel Corpus Christi; The Loud Family; Go Go Market; Vicki Randle* and many more artists. Dawn is endorsed by *Pacific Drums, Zildjian Cymbals* and *Vic Firth Sticks*.

Also by Dawn and available through Mel Bay Publications: *Beginning Rock Drum Chart; Building Blocks of Rock; Fill Workbook; Block Rockin' Beats.*

Table of Contents

**Drawings by Lori Nunokawa
Design Assistance from Alicia Buelow
Recording by Joe Gore**

Drums

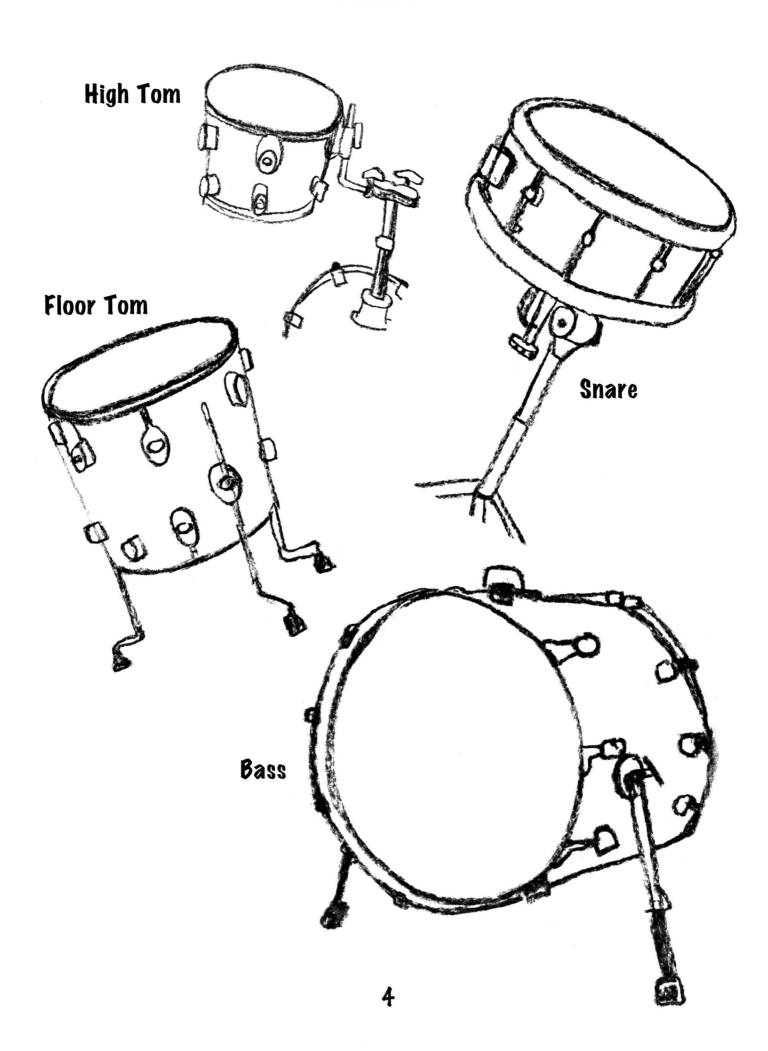

High Tom

Floor Tom

Snare

Bass

Cymbals/Hardware

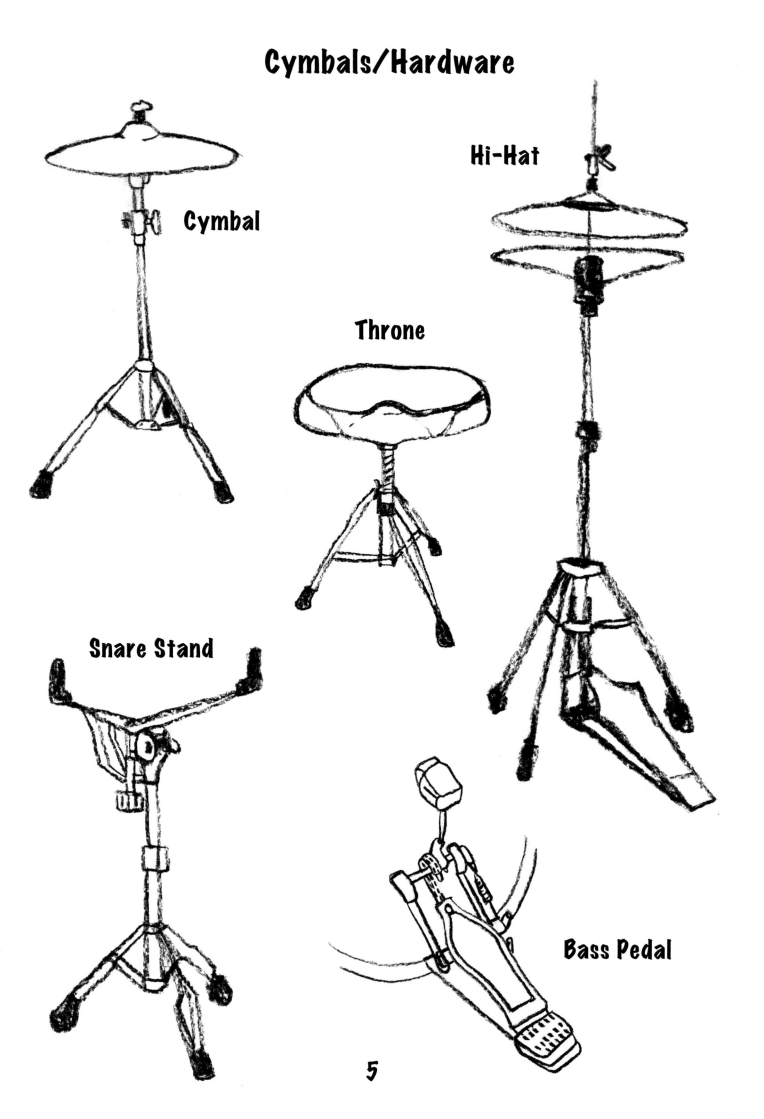

Cymbal

Hi-Hat

Throne

Snare Stand

Bass Pedal

Full Drum Kit

More Drums

Bongos

Conga

Djembe

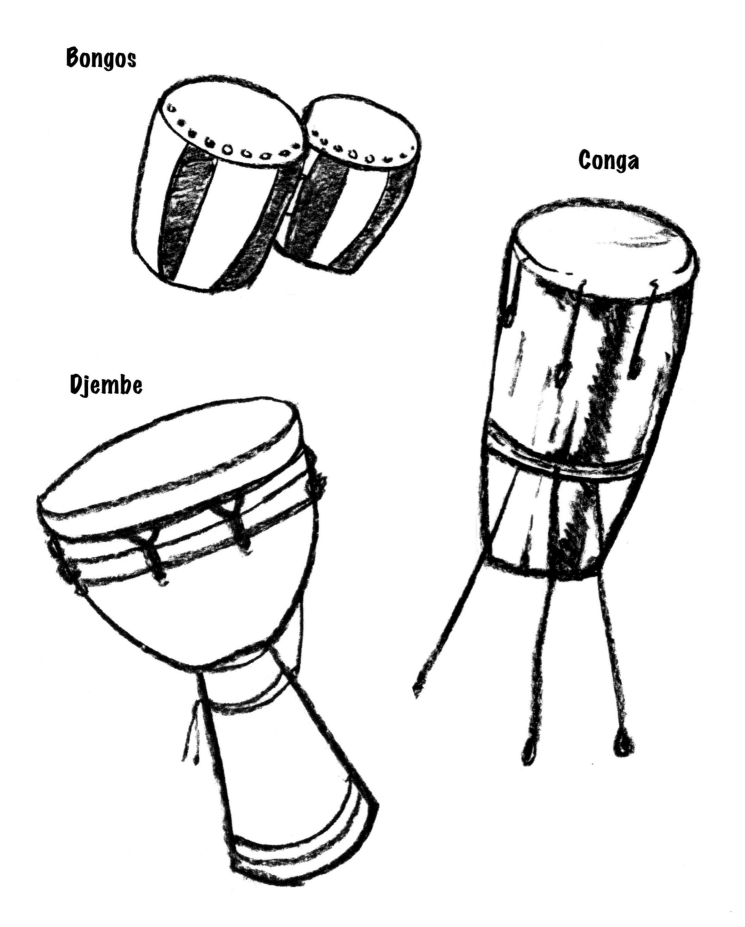

Basic Terms

This is a one-line staff.

The two numbers represent the Time Signature. The top number tells us how many beats are in each measure and the bottom number tells us which type of note gets one beat.

The two bold lines on the left of the staff are known as a "Neutral Clef". Drum notation is often written with this clef.

The type of notes on this line are quarter notes. The last symbol (squiggly line thingy) is called a quarter rest.

The smaller lines between the notes are called bar lines.

One "measure" or "bar" is between the bar lines.
Each quarter note or rest gets one count in **2/4** time.

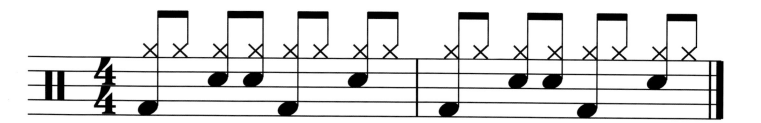

This is the five-line staff.

This staff is often used to write drum kit music.

The last two lines are a double bar line, signfying the end.

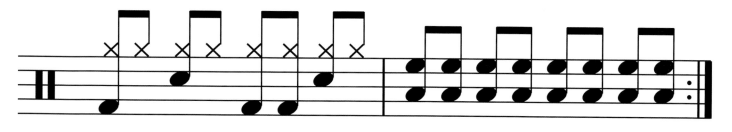

Drum Set Groove   **Tom-toms**

The last two lines are a double bar line with two dots. This is a repeat sign. For practice using this book, we usually want to repeat each exercise many times. Technically, the symbol means to repeat it just once.

Drum set notation most often uses the "x" notehead for cymbals and regular noteheads for drums.

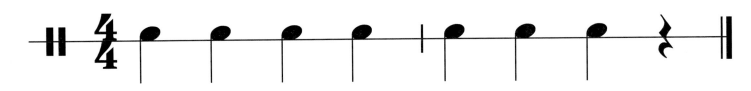

Chapter 1

This chapter explains some basic note and rest values, including the values shown above, quarter notes and rests.

This is chapter is in **4/4** time. **4** beats in each measure and a quarter note gets one count.

Watch out for the repeat signs! Play each exercise many times for practice.

Use any drum you can play with sticks or with your hands – here are some examples of drums you can use:

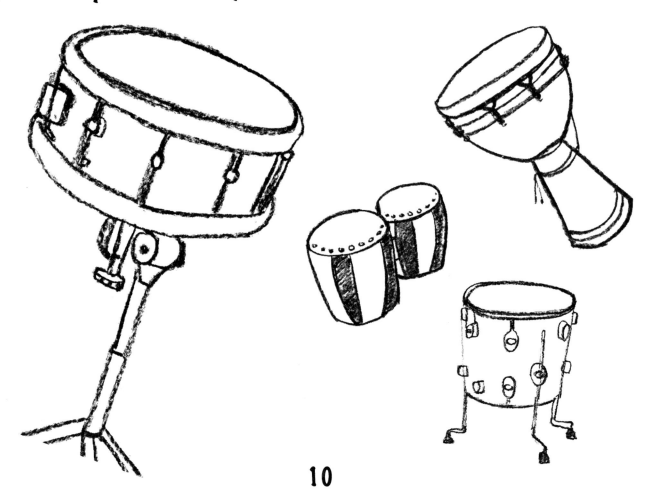

Counting is on the top and sticking is on the bottom, start slowly and work on building up your speed.

Quarter notes get one count each – repeat these many times!

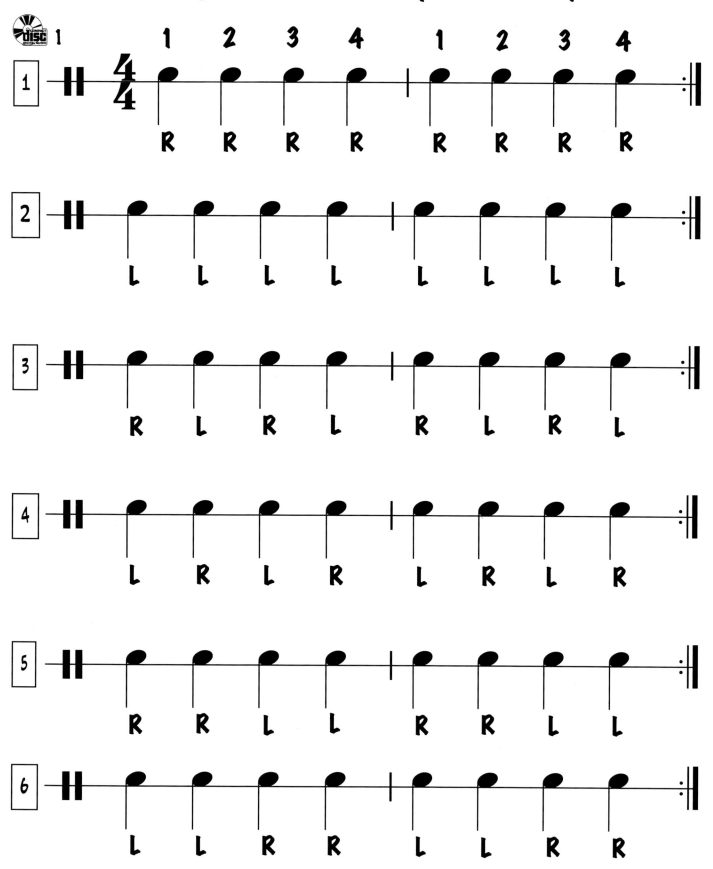

Counting Notes & Rests
Quarter notes and rests get one count each

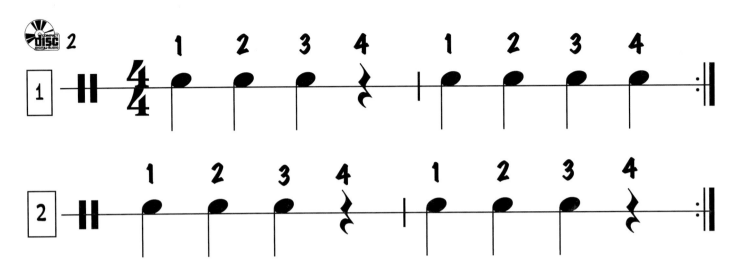

Half notes and rests get two counts each

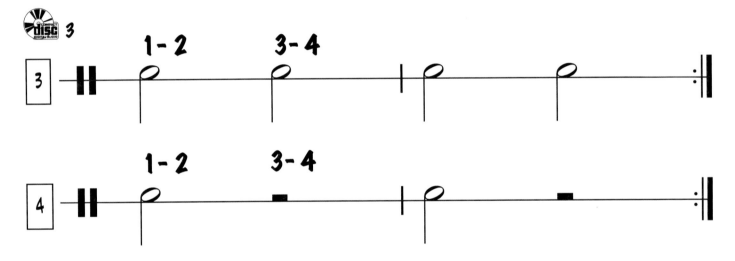

Whole notes and rests get four counts each

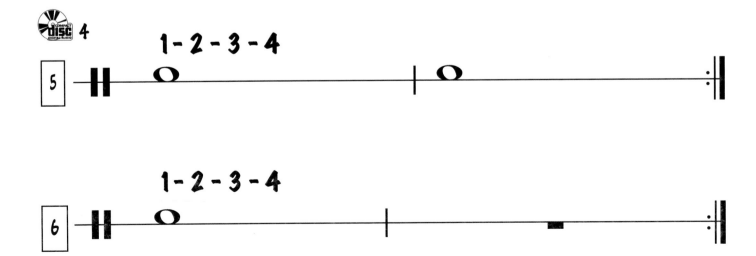

12

More with quarter notes and rests – count and play these on any drum! Write the counting on top, or count aloud.

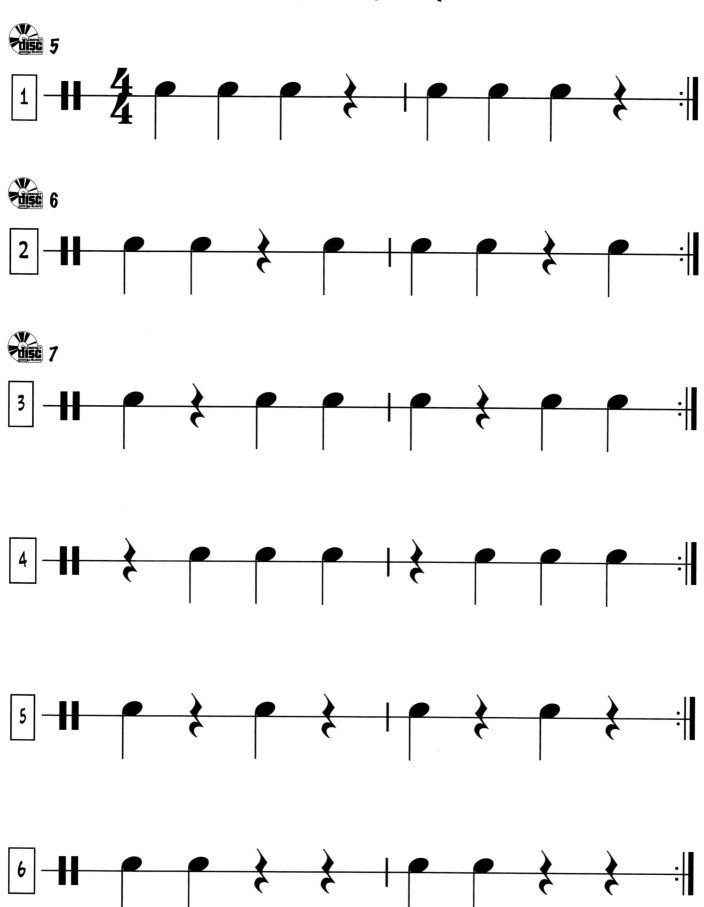

Chapter 2

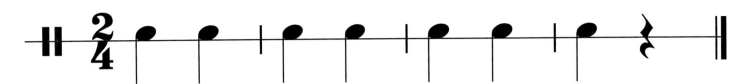

This is chapter is in **2/4** Time. **2** beats in each measure and a quarter note or rest gets one count. Try to count and play at the same time.

Play each exercise many times for practice when there are repeat signs.

Use any drum or cymbal you can play with sticks or with your hands. Try some new ones – here are some examples of drums and cymbals you might choose for this chapter:

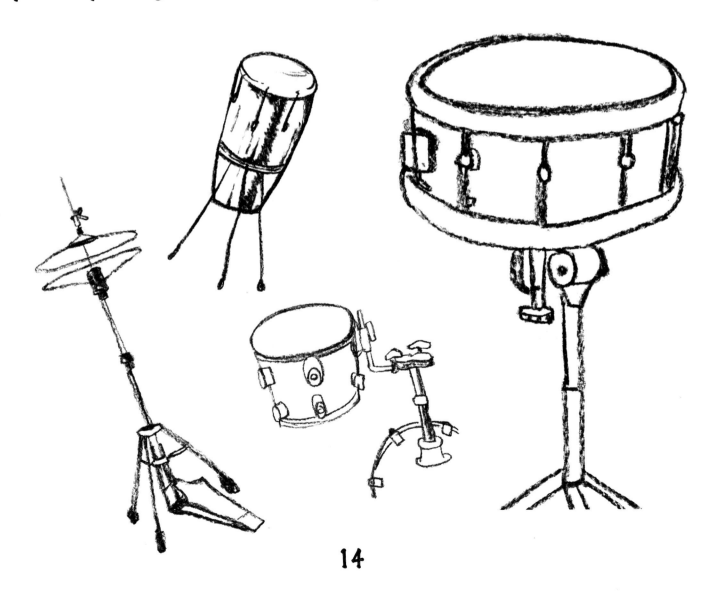

Quarter Notes and Rests in 2/4 Time
Count aloud or write the counting above the music.

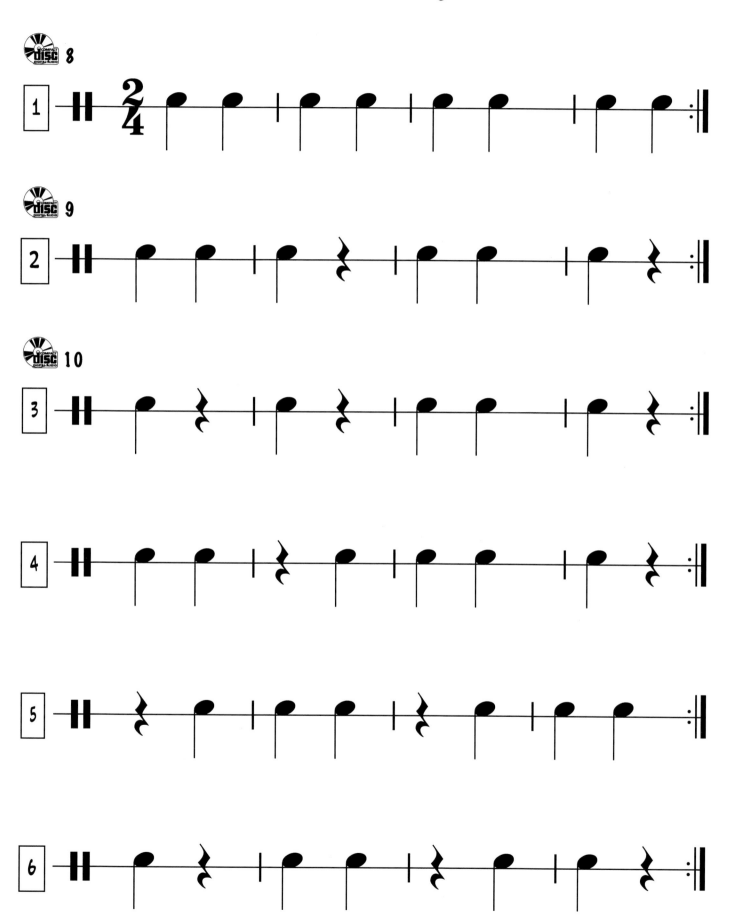

More in 2/4 time

 11

1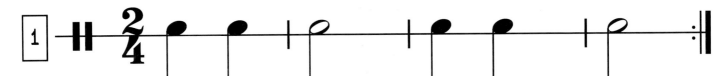

 12

2

3

4

5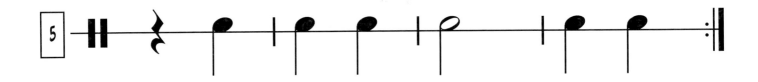

6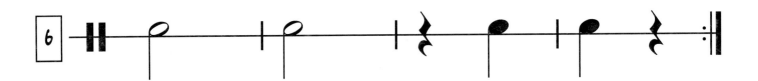

Solo in 2/4

Try to read this whole page. If you have trouble, practice each line
until you can put the whole solo together.

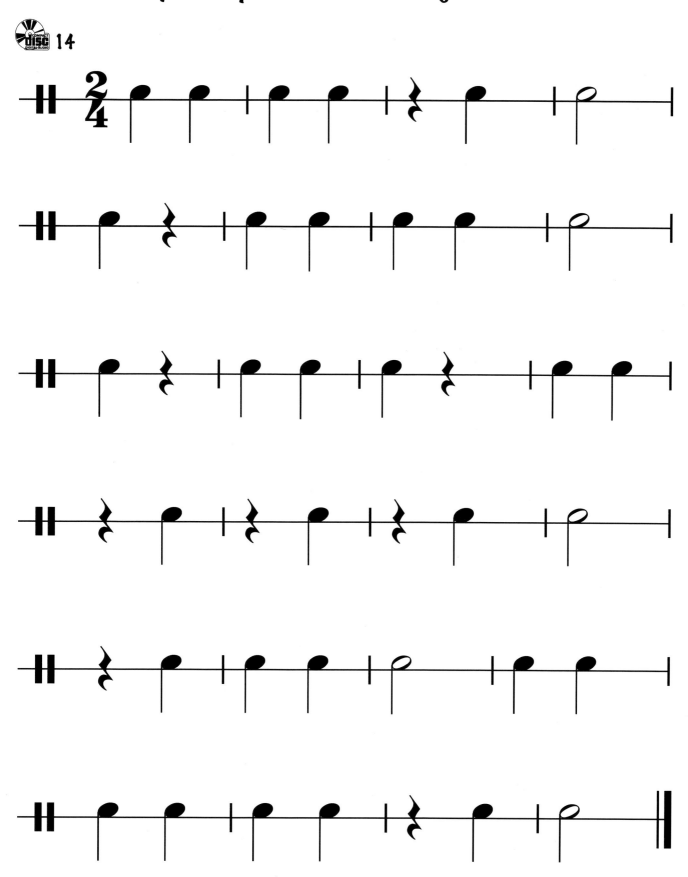

Chapter 3

This chapter is in **2/4** time. **2** Beats in each measure and a quarter note gets one count. Where the notes are on the staff tells us which drum to hit when we play beats on the drum kit. We have the instrument below the notes here to help you remember.

This is the **5** line staff that we will use to write beats for the drum kit.

Hi Hat   **Snare Drum**   **Bass Drum**

Warm ups in 2/4 time
Repeat many times and write the counting on top, if you need to.

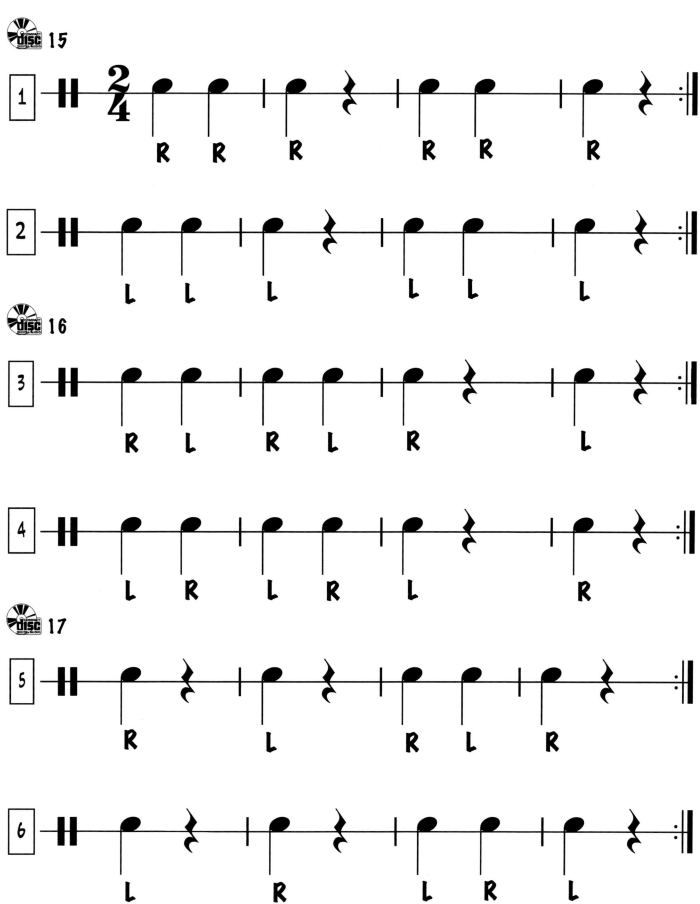

Beats in 2/4 Time

Hi Hat **Snare Drum**

Hi Hat & Snare

Hi Hat & Bass Drum

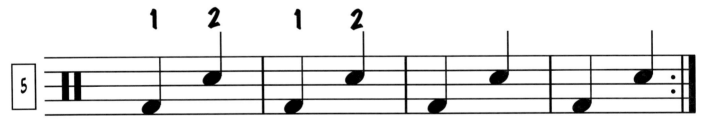

Bass & Snare

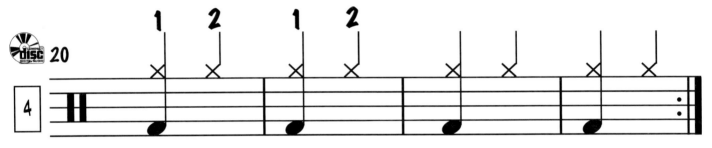

All Three Together!

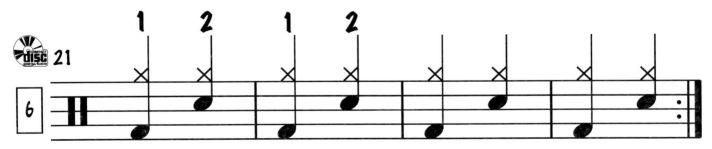

More Beats in 2/4 Time

Only Bass Drum

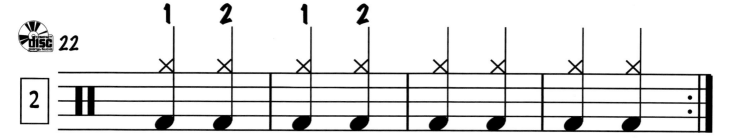

Hi Hat & Bass Drum together

22

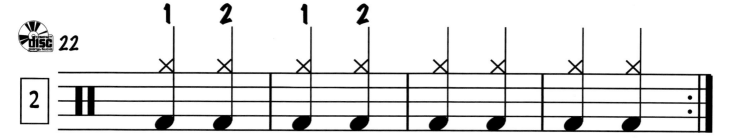

Bass & Snare

All three together

23

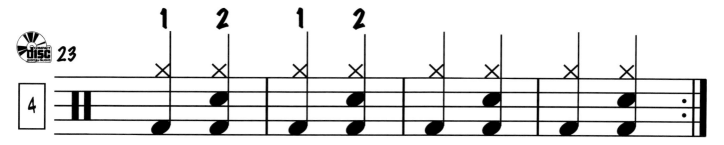

New groove!

24

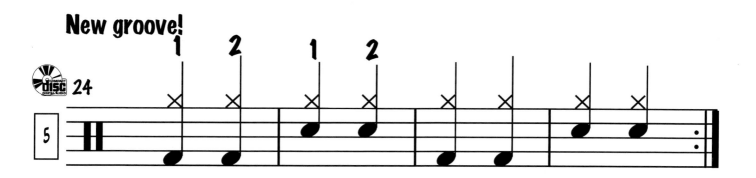

Chapter 4

Practice counting and playing in **4/4** time with the Hi Hat, below.

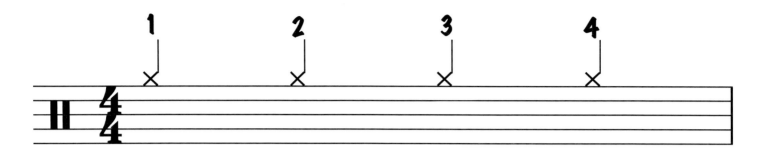

This chapter is in **4/4** time. **4** Beats in each measure and a quarter note gets one count. Count to **4** when you are playing the patterns in this chapter on the drum kit. The Rudiments are also in **4/4** time.

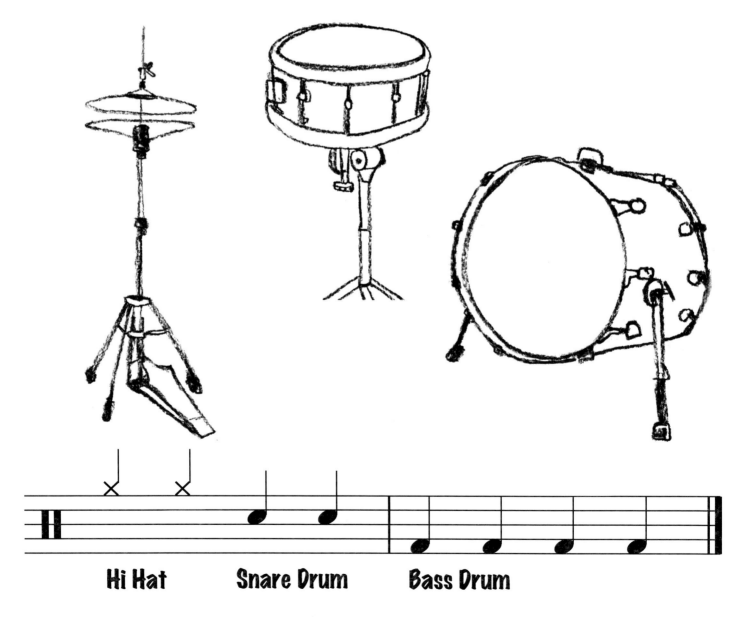

Hi Hat   Snare Drum   Bass Drum

Rudiments

These are basic elements of drumming. Repeat each one many times. Work on going faster and faster each time you practice.

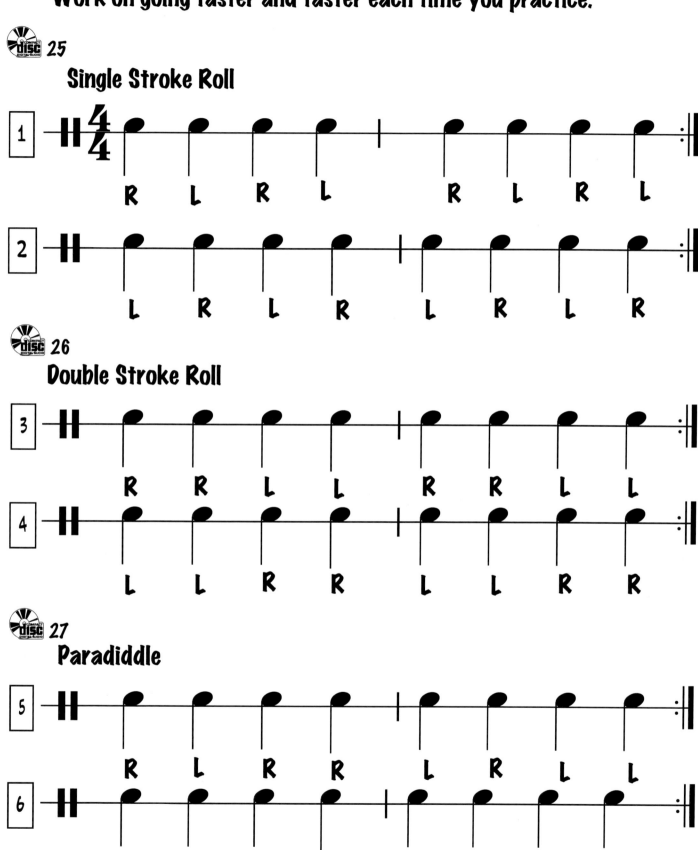

25

Single Stroke Roll

26

Double Stroke Roll

27

Paradiddle

Beats in 4/4 Time

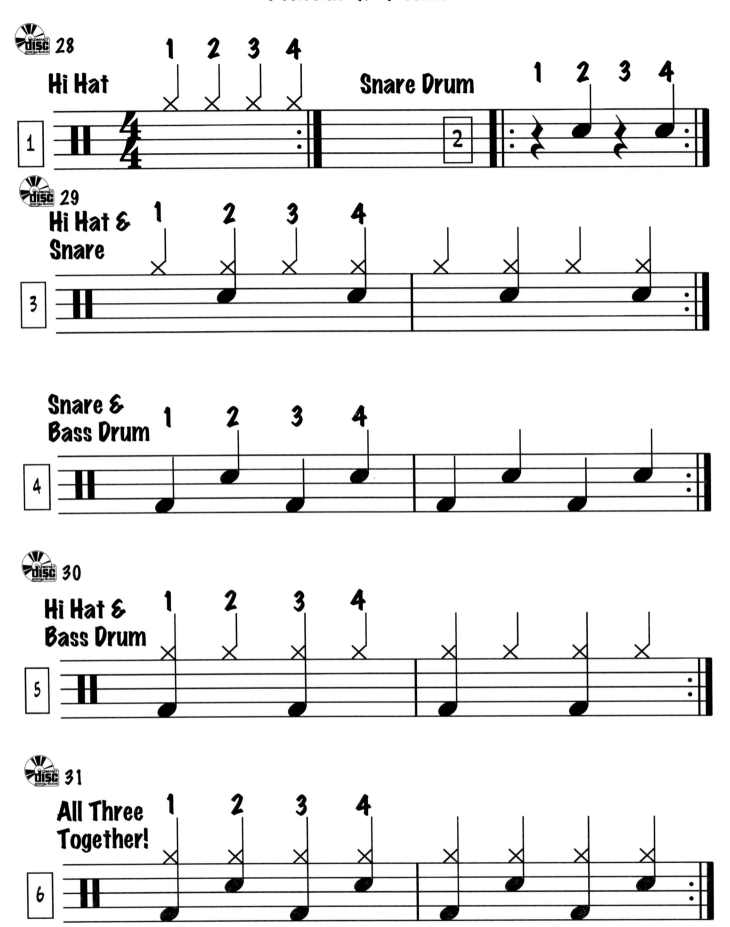

More Quarter Note Beats

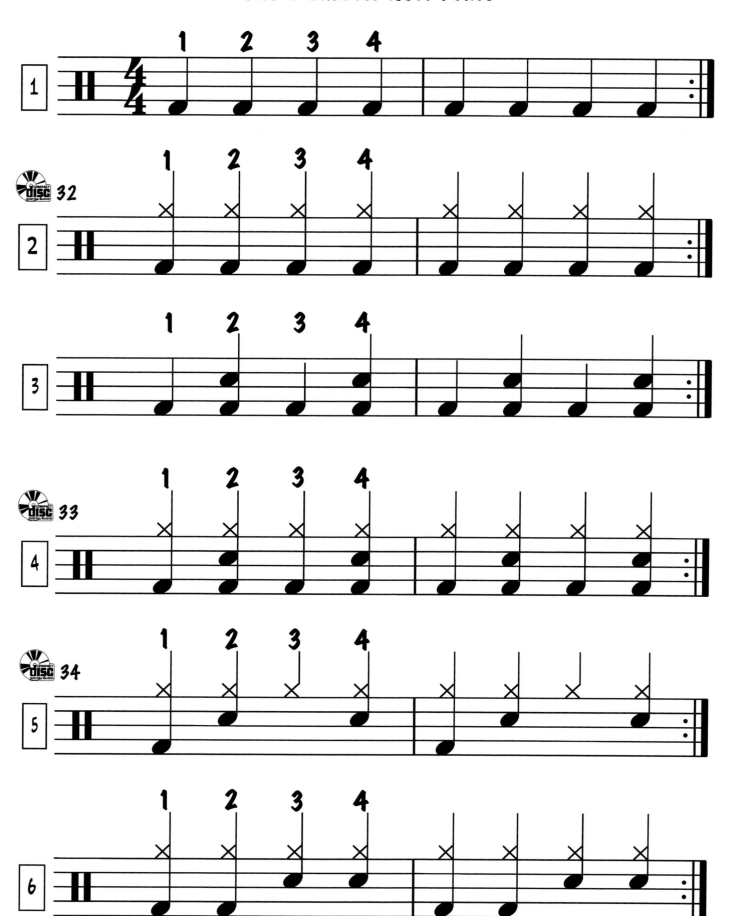

Chapter 5

This chapter introduces a new note value, the eighth note. There are two eighth notes in the space of one quarter note and we count them "One And Two And" in **2/4** time. Here is a review of note values and time signatures for the chapter. We will use both **2/4** and **4/4** time. All note values also have a matching rest value.

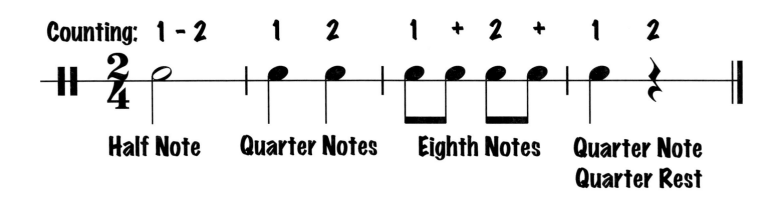

Whole Note = 4 counts
Quarter Note = 1 count

Half Note = 2 counts
Eighth Note = 1/2 count

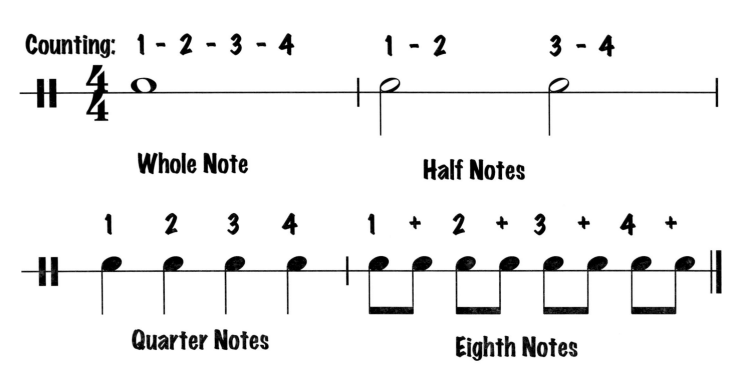

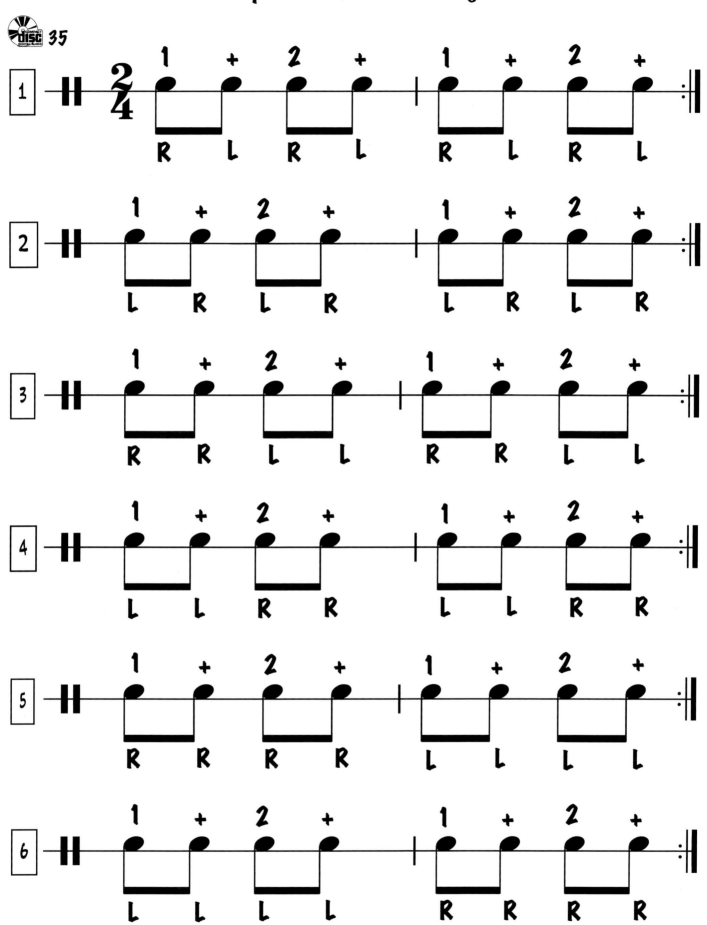

Eighth Notes
There are two eighth notes for each quarter note.

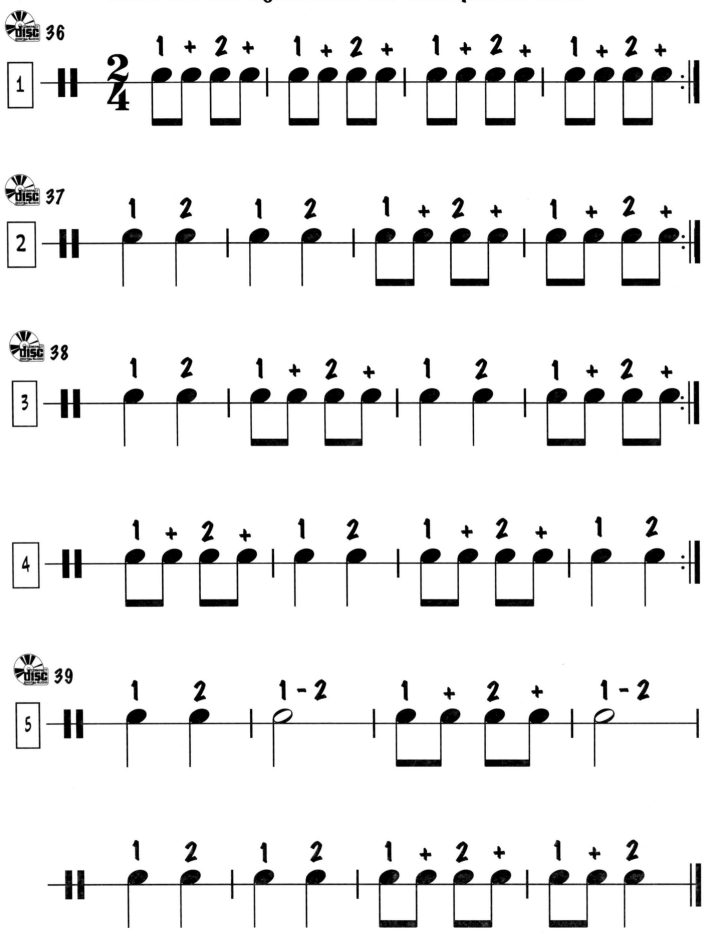

More with Eighth Notes in 4/4 time

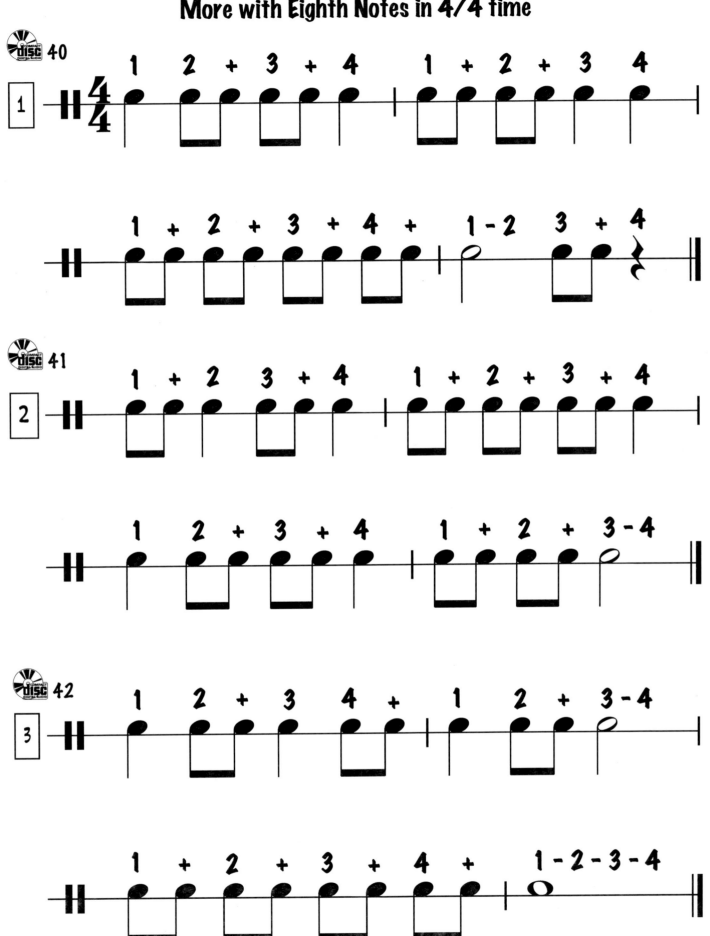

Chapter 6

This chapter we will focus on eighth notes in 2/4 time. Play the warm ups on the snare drum. Then we have beats on the drum kit using eighth notes. Remember to count "One And Two And" to help keep on track for the beats. Below we have a reminder of where the notes are on the staff for the drum kit.

Hi Hat   **Snare Drum**   **Bass Drum**

Warm ups in 2/4 time

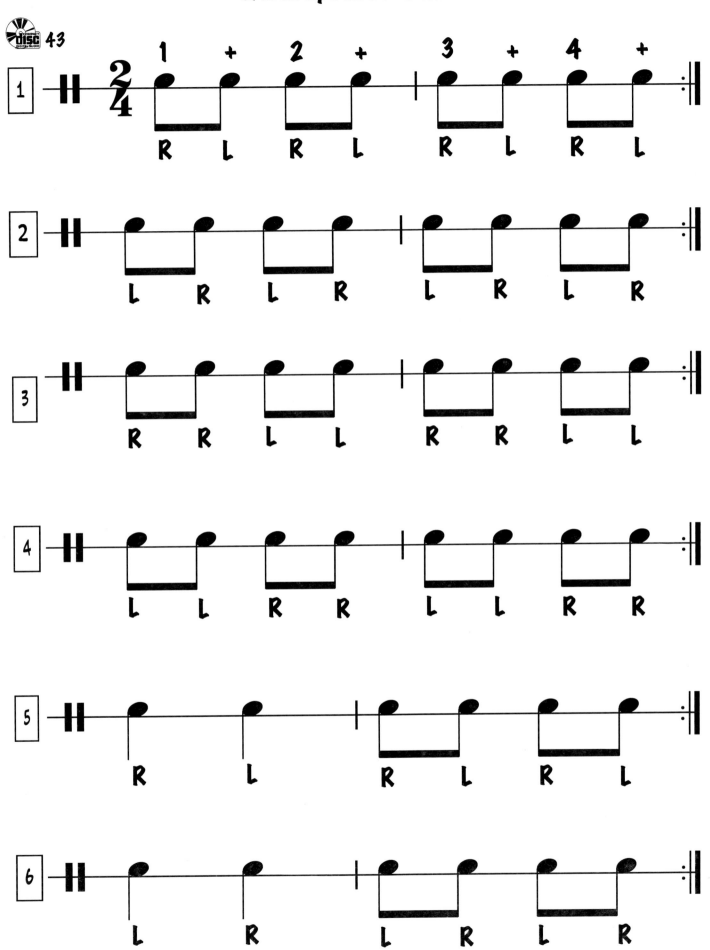

Eighth Notes on the Drum Kit

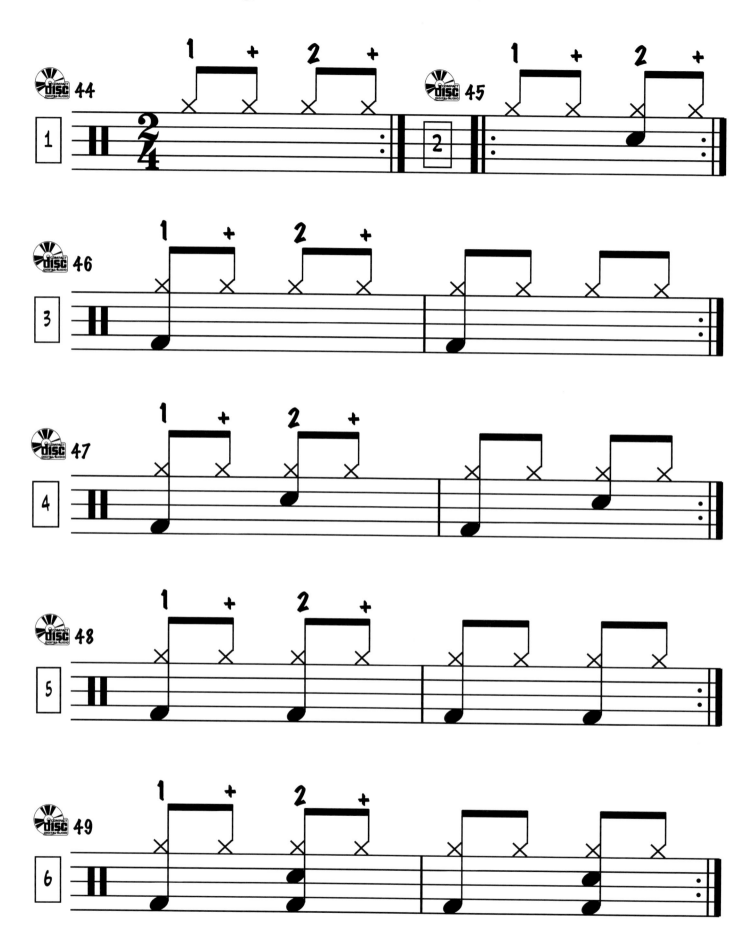

More Eighth Note Beats

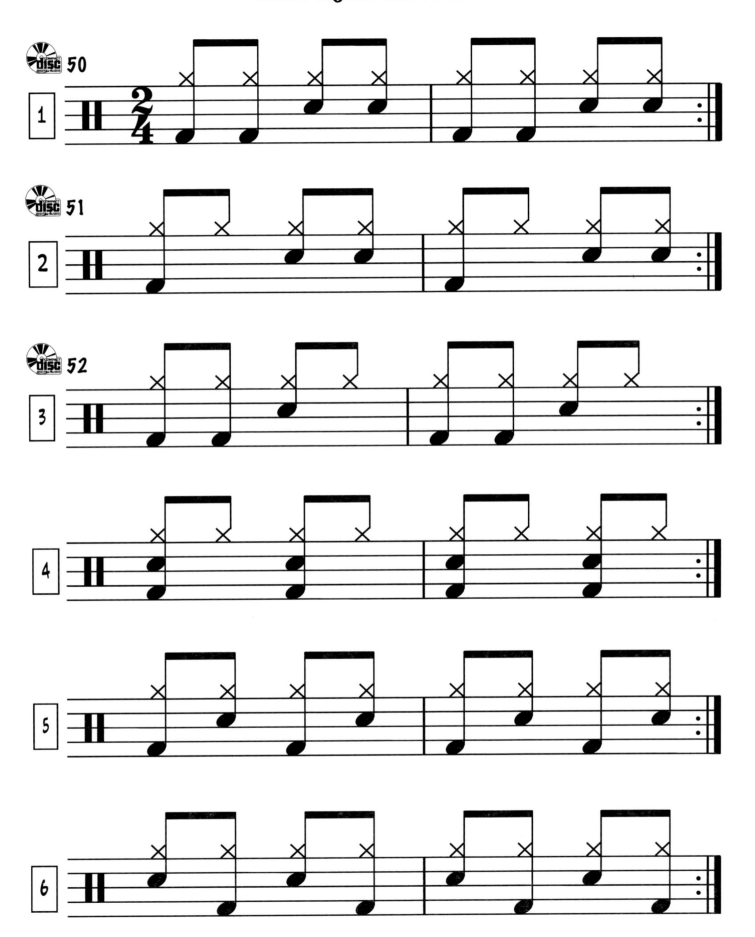

Chapter 7

This is chapter is in **3/4** time. 3 beats in each measure and a quarter note/rest gets one count. Play this chapter on the snare drum.

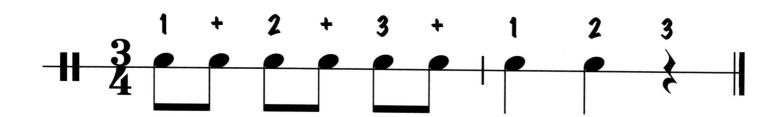

We have some new symbols and dynamic markings in this chapter.

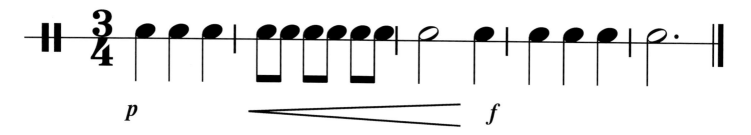

p stands for "piano" and means play soft

f stands for "forte" and means play loud

Crescendo means to get louder gradually and looks like this:

This is a one bar repeat sign. It means to repeat the measure right before this: ∕.

Note value review in **3/4** time:

Dotted Half Note = 3 counts   Half Note = 2 counts
Quarter Notes = 1 count   Eighth Notes = 1/2 count

Warm Ups in 3/4 Time

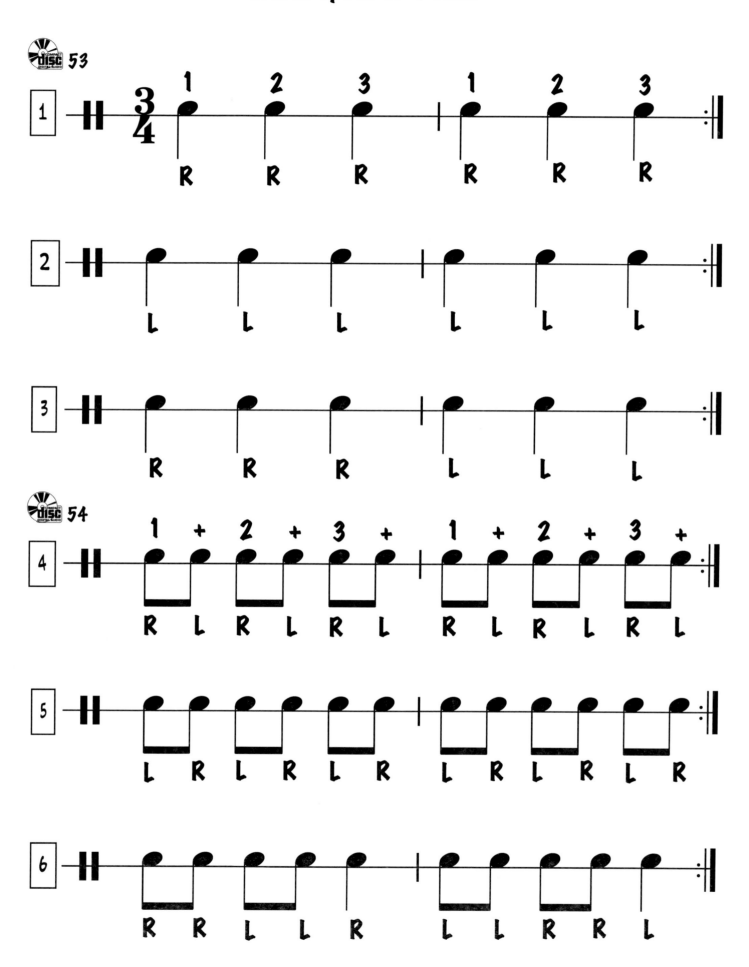

More New Musical Symbols

Dotted Notes: A dot after a note always ads one half of that note's value back to the note. A dotted half note would get three beats in **3/4** time. The one measure repeat is used to tell you to repeat the measure right before this symbol one more time. It looks like this: ./.

Solo in 3/4 Time

Write the counting on top if you need to and watch for new symbols and dynamics. Crescendo means to get louder gradually and looks like this: ⟨

Chapter 8

Practice counting and playing beats with eighth notes in **4/4** time.
Play the warm ups on any drum on the kit to start.

Hi Hat   **Snare Drum**   **Bass Drum**

Warm Ups with Eighth Notes

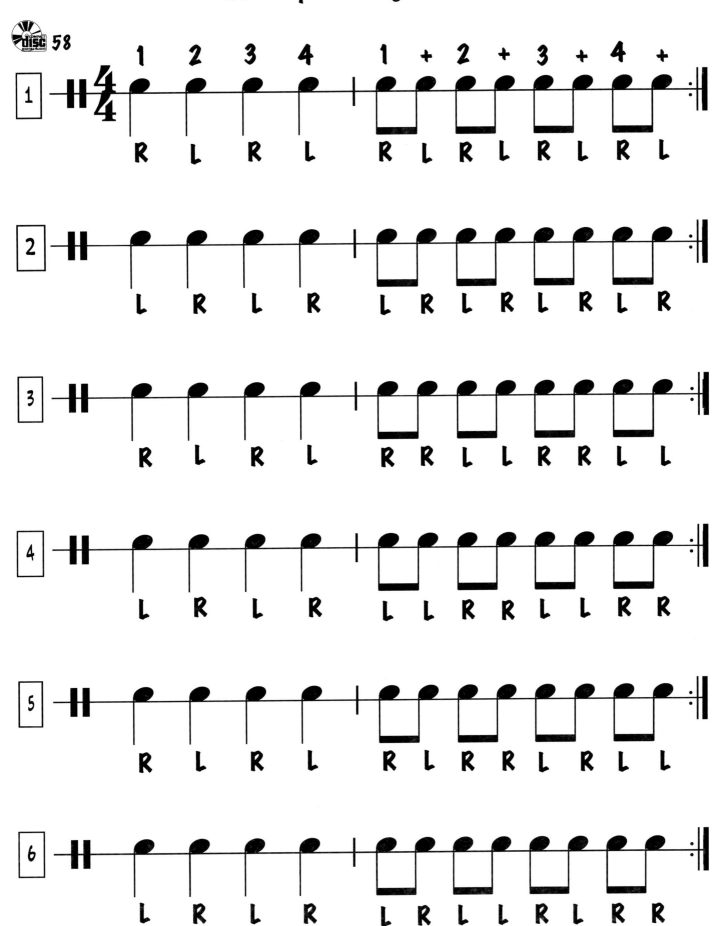

Eighth Note Beats in 4/4 Time

More Beats with Eighth Notes

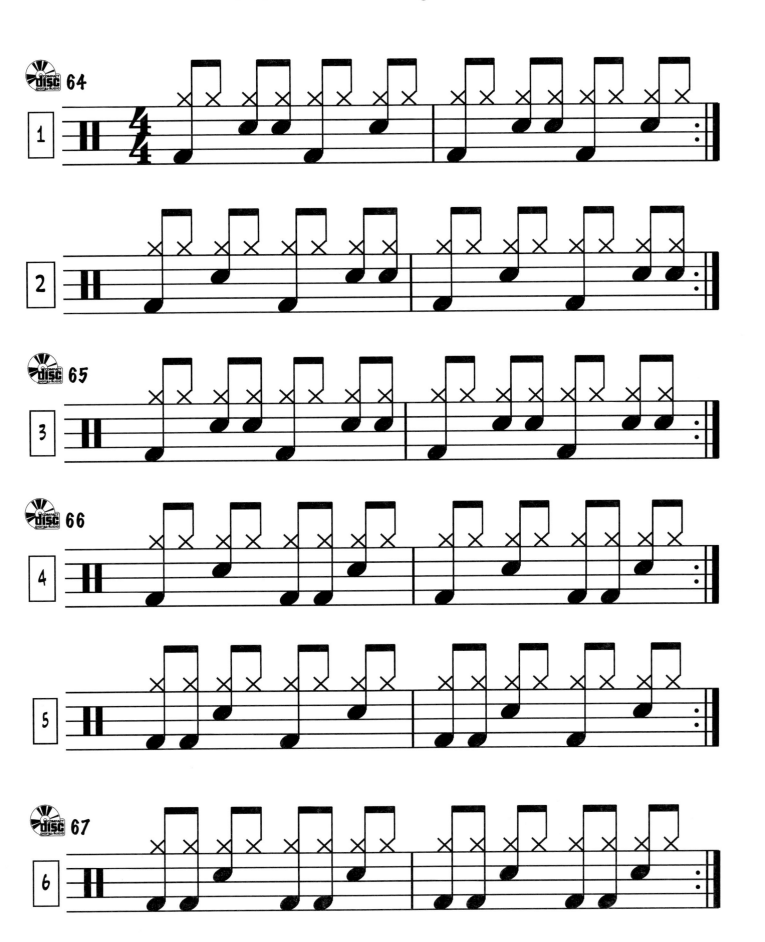

Chapter 9

This chapter has more grooves in **4/4** time and some new warm ups with dynamics.

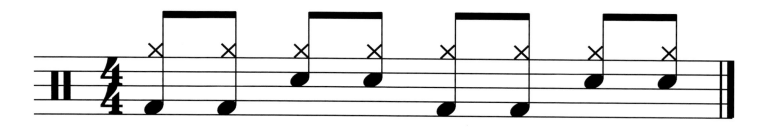

There are some new dynamics in the warm up section. Below is a key with both new and old dynamic markings.

p stands for "piano" and means play soft

mp stands for "mezzo piano" and means play medium soft

mf stands for "mezzo forte" and means play medium loud

f stands for "forte" and means play loud

Warm Ups with Dynamics
This means first time through soft, second time loud: *p - f*

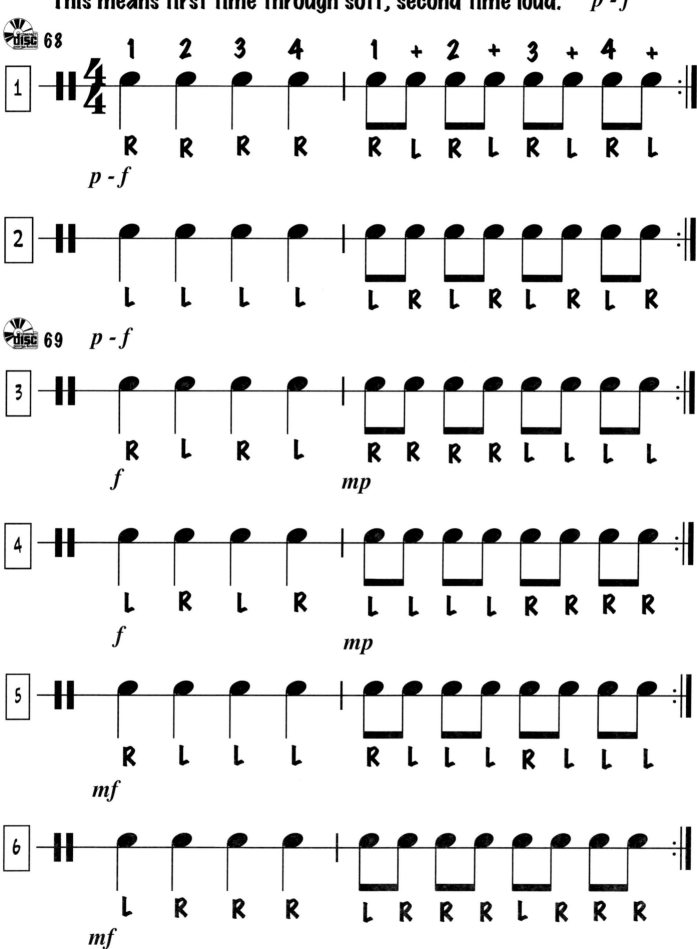

More Beats with Eighth Notes

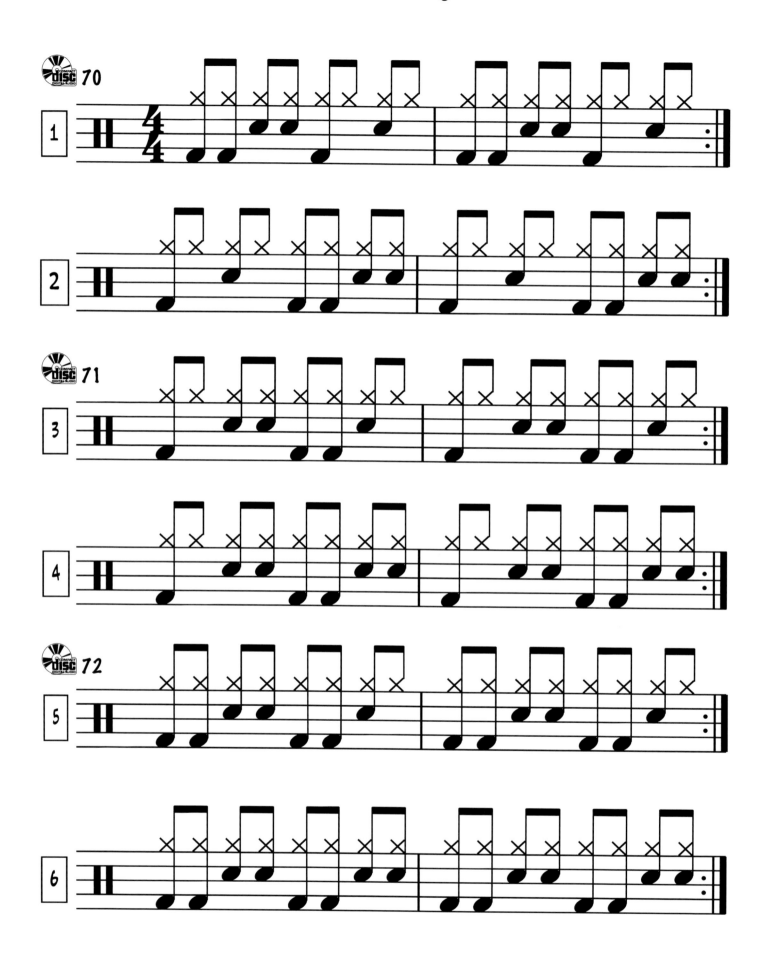

Two Bar Patterns – watch for changes in bar two!

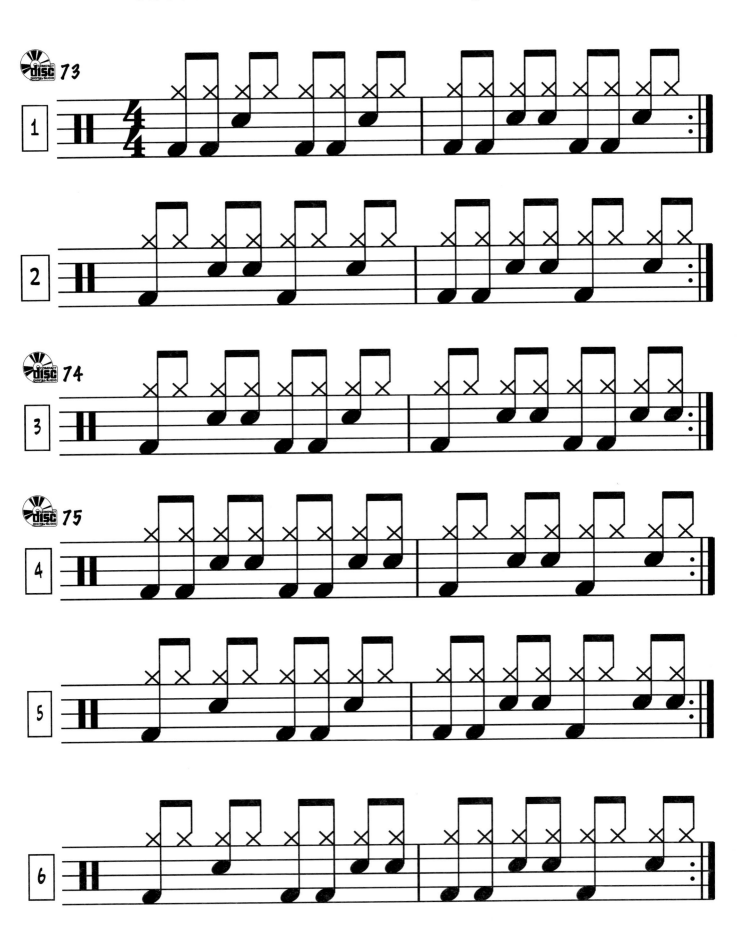

45

Chapter 10

Now we are going to play on the tom-toms. The top space on the staff is the high tom; the third space down means low tom. Both notes means play the hands together.

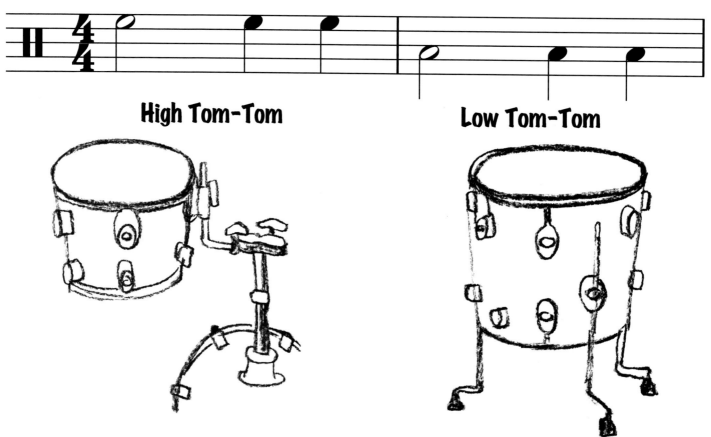

High Tom-Tom   Low Tom-Tom

Just like the eighth note, the eighth rest gets 1/2 count. In the first example, the rest is on the "and" or on the "off beat". The second example has the rest on the numbers, also called the "downbeat". Play hands together – both toms.

Count: 1 + 2 + 3 + 4 +   1 + 2 + 3 + 4 +

Hands Together on the Tom-Toms
Watch the dynamics!

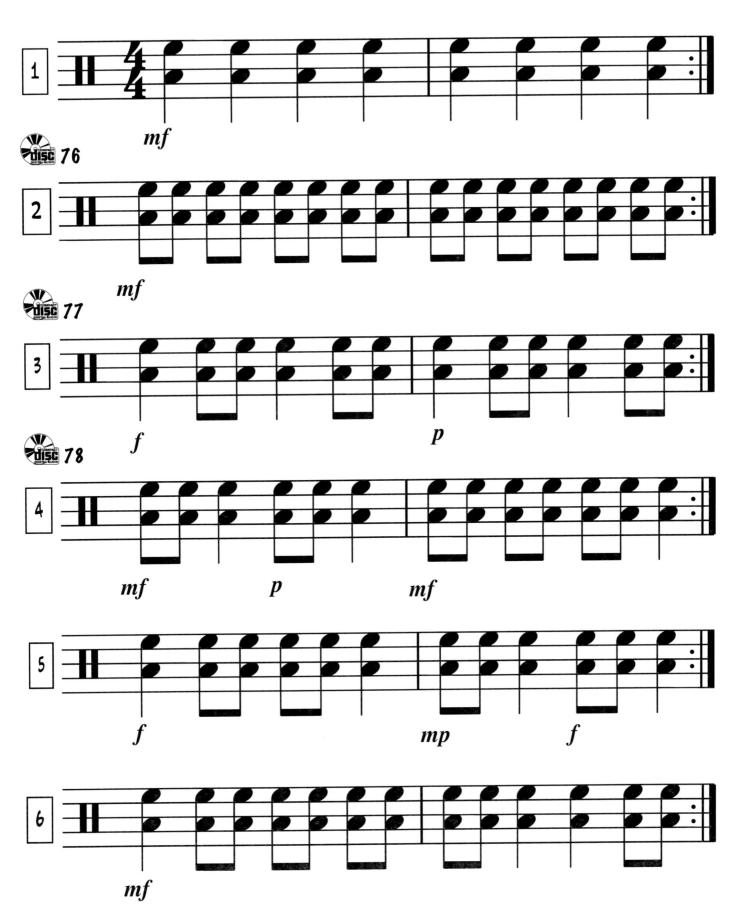

47

The Eighth Rest

Just like the eighth note, the eighth rest gets 1/2 count.

More with the Eighth Rest

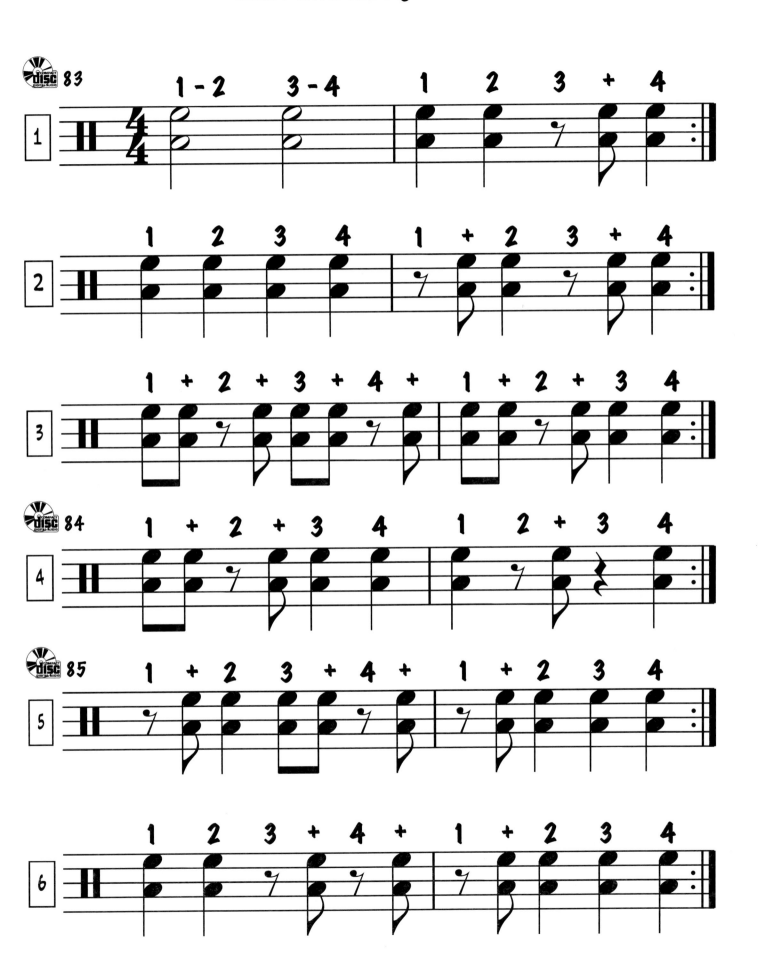

Chapter 11

Rudiments are basic elements of drumming. We started these in Chapter 4 with the single-stroke roll, double-stroke roll and the paradiddle. This chapter has 4 more essential rudiments. Work on going faster each time you practice. Some of the rudiments include a new symbol called an accent (>).That means to make that note louder than the other notes.

This chapter also has new drum kit beats and beats with syncopation, like the pattern below. Syncopation means to accentuate the weaker beats - the "off-beats" or "ands".

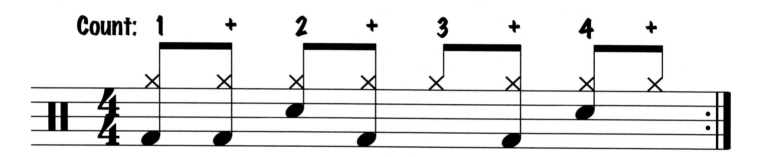

We end the book with 4 bar phrases with fills. Usually we play fills for the transitions between sections of the songs. Have fun!

Rudiments

 86

Double Paradiddle

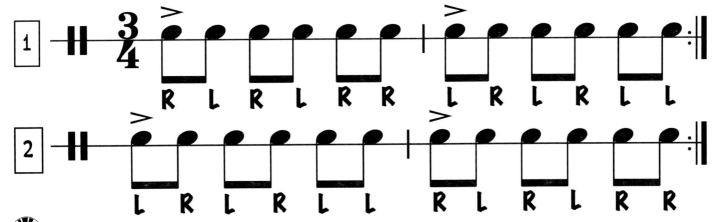

 87

5 Stroke Roll

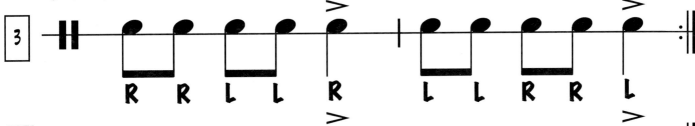

 88

7 Stroke Roll

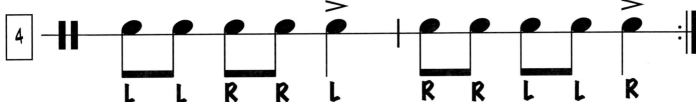

 89

Flam

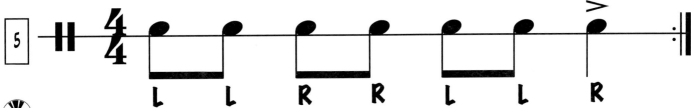

More Beats

2 Bar Combinations

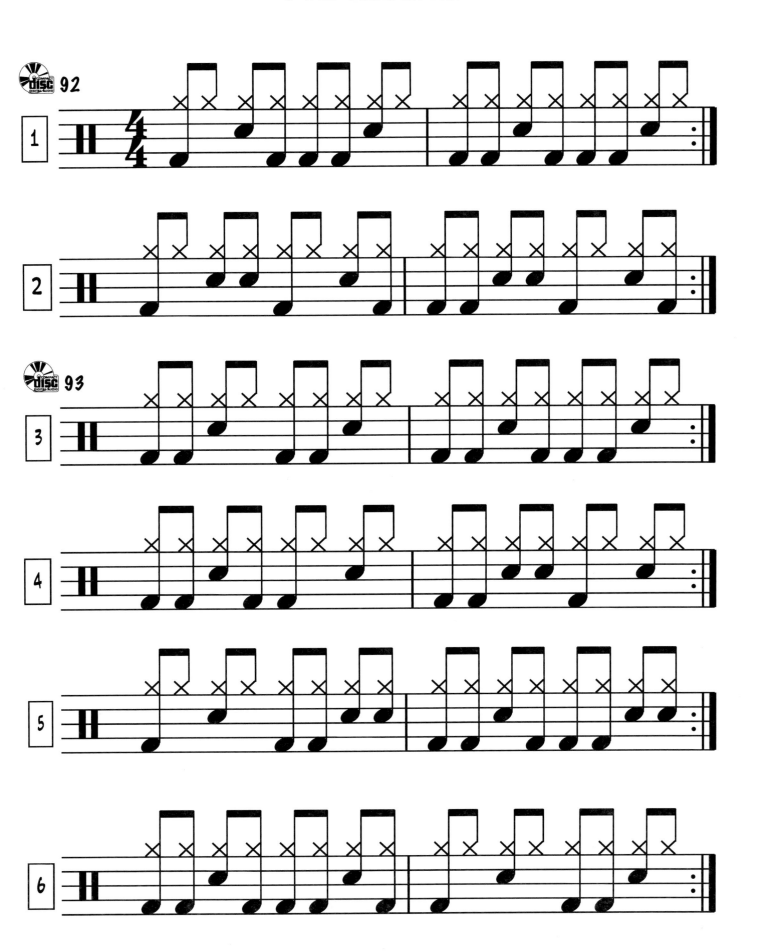

Beats with Syncopation

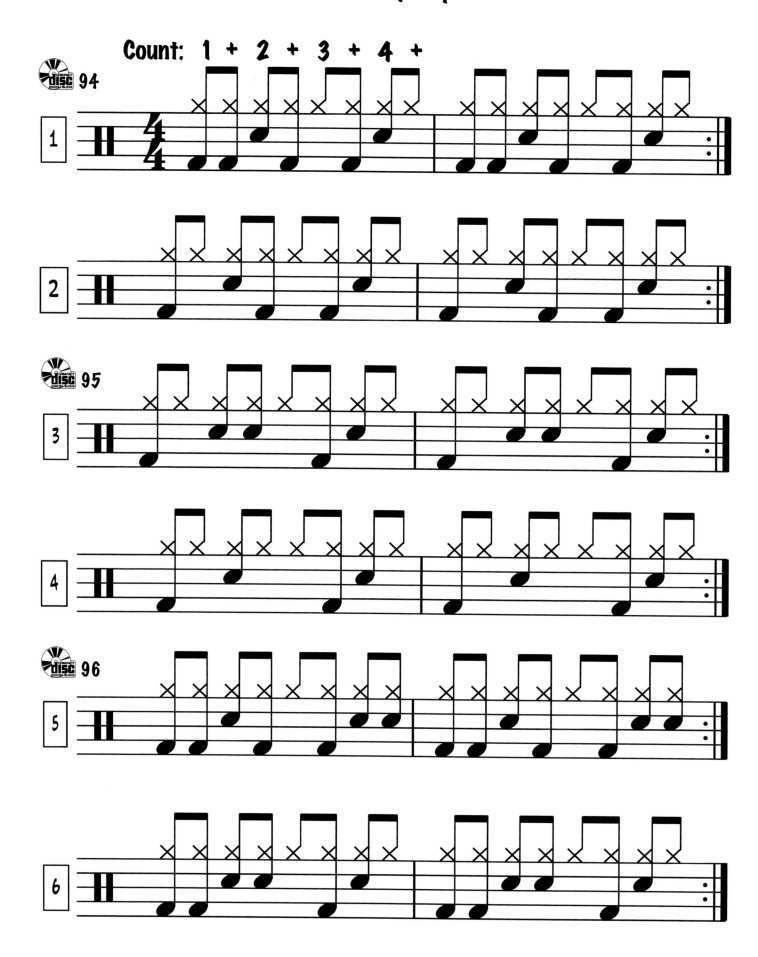

4 Bar Phrases with 1 Bar Fills

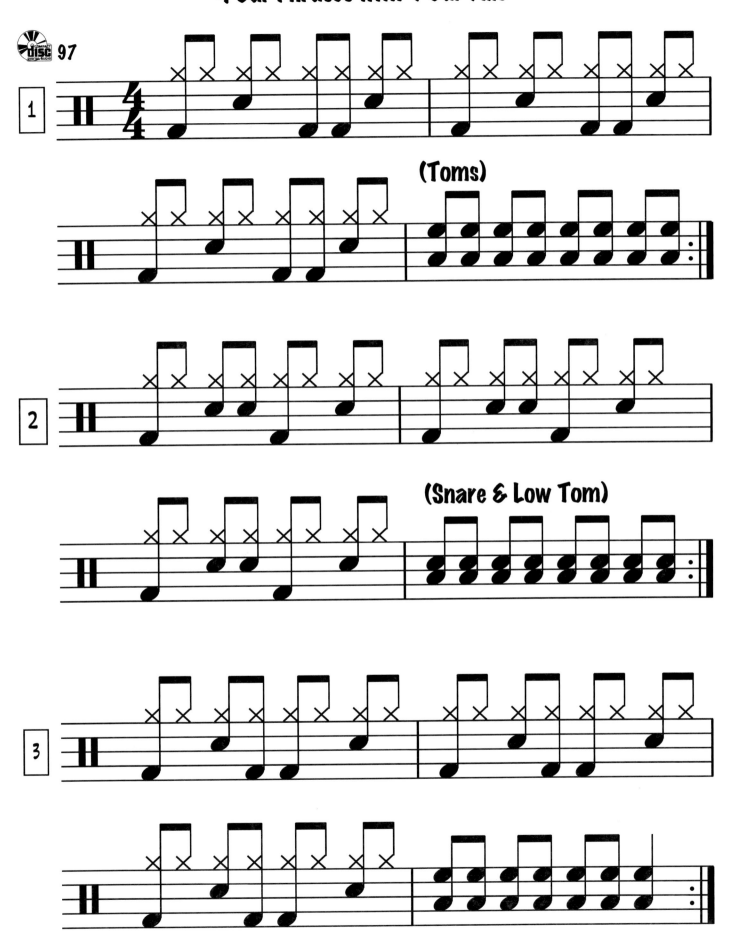

(Toms)

(Snare & Low Tom)

4 Bar Phrases with 1/2 Bar Fills

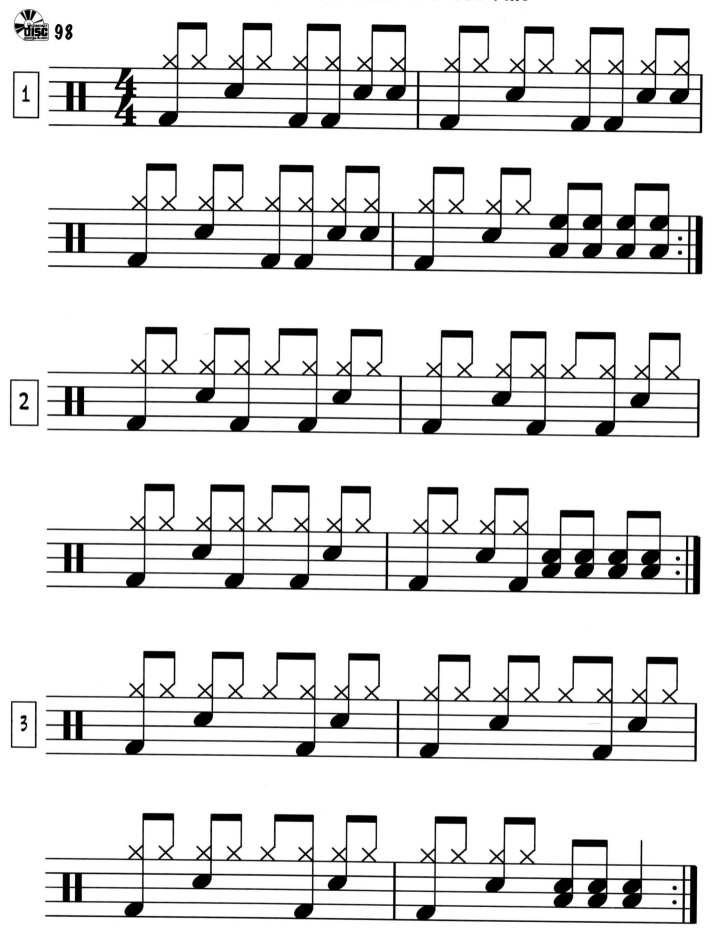